RANDY BULLIS

Beginners Guide to Tracing Your Roots

First Steps to Starting a Family Tree

First published by Mixtli Publishing 2024

Copyright © 2024 by Randy Bullis

All rights reserved. No part of this publication may be reproduced, stored or transmitted in any form or by any means, electronic, mechanical, photocopying, recording, scanning, or otherwise without written permission from the publisher. It is illegal to copy this book, post it to a website, or distribute it by any other means without permission.

Randy Bullis asserts the moral right to be identified as the author of this work.

Randy Bullis has no responsibility for the persistence or accuracy of URLs for external or third-party Internet Websites referred to in this publication and does not guarantee that any content on such Websites is, or will remain, accurate or appropriate.

Designations used by companies to distinguish their products are often claimed as trademarks. All brand names and product names used in this book and on its cover are trade names, service marks, trademarks and registered trademarks of their respective owners. The publishers and the book are not associated with any product or vendor mentioned in this book. None of the companies referenced within the book have endorsed the book.

First edition

This book was professionally typeset on Reedsy.
Find out more at reedsy.com

To my lovely wife Molly, who has encouraged me for 25 years to write.

Contents

	Foreword	ii
1	Chapter One – Introduction	1
2	Chapter Two – Getting Started	6
3	Chapter Three – Putting Your Research in Order	11
4	Chapter Four – Online Resources	14
5	Chapter Five – Visiting Archives and Libraries	20
6	Chapter Six – DNA Testing	24
7	Chapter Seven – Overcoming Challenges	31
8	Chapter 8 – Preserving Family History	35
9	Chapter 9 – Continuing Education	40
10	Chapter 10 – Reflections and Gratitude	44
11	APPENDIX	47

Foreword

I was raised by a single mother. My biological father was out of the picture at an early age, and he died when I was about eight, so I did not have any real contact with my father's side of the family, and I knew very little about him or my extended family on that side. My questions to my mom were often answered with "I don't remember" or "I just don't know." Since I grew up in Texas and my paternal family was in Michigan, I had no way of reaching out. This was way before the days of the internet.

I spent a lot of time as a young man writing letters to anyone named Bullis in the Michigan area, hoping that someone would eventually answer me. One day, when I was in my mid-twenties, I received a letter from Howard Bullis, who lived in Florida. He was asking me for information about the Bullis side of the family. Having no clue about any of that information, I wrote back, saying that all I knew was my father's name and the fact that he was from Michigan.

Six weeks later, I received in the mail some information that would start a passion for family history that I did not know I had. Howard, a distant cousin, sent me information on my father's side that went back several generations. With that data, I was able to reach out and make contact with my grandfather's sister. She had been looking for me for several years.

As tools for assisting in a search for my roots became more and more available, I was able to find not only my father's side but also family members in Mexico from my mother's side of the family.

I hope that this guide can provide you with the tools to start your search. This is not meant to be a comprehensive guide, but rather a way to put you on the path to the discovery of your family legacy. I hope that you find as much pleasure in finding your roots as I have over the last 40 years.

1

Chapter One - Introduction

To forget one's ancestors is to be a brook without a source, a tree without a root. – **Chinese Proverb**

What is genealogy?

Understanding one's ancestry in depth is possible through studying and tracking familial lines and relationships, which is what genealogy entails. The word refers to the investigation of the biological, cultural, and social ties that unite generations rather than merely enumerating names and dates. Fundamentally, the goal of genealogy is to trace a person's lineage and reveal the stories buried in the past that can illuminate the present.

Investigating one's ancestry requires careful study, drawing on archives, historical documents, and oral traditions that have been passed down over the years. It promotes an understanding of interconnected lives by extending beyond biological links to include adopted or stepfamily members. Using a variety of resources, such as family trees, records, images, and DNA testing, genealogists create a compelling story about the development of families.

Genealogy is extremely important since it provides a strong sense of self and community. It makes it possible for people to value their cultural history, ancestry, and the hardships and victories of their ancestors. In the end, researching one's ancestry can help one feel more connected to their heritage and have a greater understanding of the different threads that together make up human history by acting as a link between the past and present.

The importance of exploring one's family history

Tracing one's ancestry holds significant importance for several reasons:

1. Cultural and Identity Connection: Having a solid understanding of one's lineage helps one connect to their cultural heritage. It promotes a sense of recognition and belonging by helping people appreciate the traditions, practices, and values that have been handed down through the ages. Although I've always felt connected to my mother's Mexican origins, I was unaware of my beginnings in Canada, the Northeast Coast, and eventually England.
2. Personal Identity and Self-Discovery: Learning more about one's ancestry can help with these concepts. It enables people to discover how their family history has shaped their personality, values, and perspective. Learning about one's family history and accomplishments might lead to better self-awareness.
3. Preserving Family History: Documenting ancestral history is a necessary step in tracing genealogy. This history must be preserved for the benefit of future generations to pre-

CHAPTER ONE - INTRODUCTION

vent the stories, experiences, and legacies of predecessors from being lost to time. It establishes a feeling of legacy and continuation.

4. Medical Insights: When combined with DNA testing, ancestry research can offer important information about possible genetic predispositions and health risks. This information will facilitate making educated healthcare decisions and taking preventative action.
5. Relationship with Extended Family: Contacting relatives of one's extended family is a common step in the genealogy research process. Reestablishing ties with family members can improve ties within the family and promote a sense of belonging and community.
6. Educational and Historical Understanding: Learning about one's ancestry helps one have a deeper comprehension of historical occurrences and societal shifts that may have influenced the course of a family. It puts people's lives in perspective within the greater context of history.
7. Sense of Continuity: Having a strong sense of one's ancestry helps one feel connected to future generations. It fosters a sense of obligation to uphold family values and traditions by assisting people in realizing the hardships, successes, and tenacity of their ancestors.
8. Satisfying Curiosity and Fostering Interest: People are inherently curious about their origins. This curiosity is satisfied, and a sense of wonder about the past is fostered by tracing lineage, which encourages a lifelong interest in history and heritage.

Discovering one's lineage is an elaborate procedure that helps people connect to their history while also enhancing their present and future by giving them a better grasp of their identity and origins.

Overview of the beginner's guide

This beginner's guide to genealogy is designed to assist individuals who are just starting their journey into exploring their family history. Here's an overview of key components in this guide.

1. **Setting Goals and Expectations:** This guide will help with defining your personal goals for family history research and setting realistic expectations for the scope of your research.
2. **Gathering Basic Information**: You will discover techniques for collecting essential information from immediate family members and conducting interviews to gather anecdotes, stories, and details.
3. **Organizing Research**: An introduction to creating a family tree and establishing an organized filing system for documents, photographs, and notes.
4. **Utilizing Online Resources**: How you can use popular genealogy websites (e.g., Ancestry.com, MyHeritage, FamilySearch) and utilize online databases and records for research.
5. **Visiting Archives and Libraries**: How can you explore local and national archives and how to access governmental records and historical archives.
6. **Introduction to DNA Testing**: Understanding the basics of DNA testing for genealogy, selecting a suitable DNA testing service, and interpreting results.

CHAPTER ONE - INTRODUCTION

7. **Overcoming Challenges:** Common Obstacles in Genealogical Research and Strategies to Overcome Them. Encouragement for persistence and patience in the face of challenges.
8. **Documenting** Findings: Creating a research log to track progress. Recording sources and citations for future reference.
9. **Preserving Family History:** Tips on Creating a Family Archive. Suggestions for digitizing photographs, documents, and preserving stories.
10. **Sharing with Relatives**: Ideas for sharing genealogical findings with family members. Hosting family reunions or creating a family newsletter or website.
11. **Continuing Education:** Encouragement to stay informed through genealogy conferences and workshops. Resources for staying updated on new research methods and tools.

2

Chapter Two - Getting Started

"Begin at the beginning," the King said very gravely, "and go on till you come to the end; then stop."
— **Lewis Carroll, *Alice in Wonderland***

Goals and Expectations

For anyone starting a genealogy journey, the first step is to set clear expectations and goals. When setting objectives and managing expectations in the course of family history research, there are a lot of things to keep in mind.

Describe your motivation for becoming interested in genealogy in detail. Is it to preserve family history, learn about cultural legacy, or find biological roots? Or is it a combination of any of the three? How thoroughly you describe your purpose will dictate the breadth and direction of your study.

Make sure you set reasonable goals. Remember the adage about how you eat an elephant—one bite at a time? Don't expect that you can find 10 generations of your family in a week. Divide the goals of your genealogical study into small, doable tasks.

CHAPTER TWO - GETTING STARTED

Setting realistic targets aids in keeping motivation and focus, whether the task is tracking a particular lineage, locating a certain ancestor, or recording an extended family's movements. Part of setting a realistic target is to set research area priorities. Decide which branches or ancestors in your family tree you want to prioritize. This helps one make efficient use of their time and resources and prevents them from becoming overwhelmed by the scope of genealogy research. Once you begin the satisfying process of doing family research, you may find yourself looking at a large number of family lines. Remember, you have two sets of grandparents, four sets of great-grandparents, eight sets of great-great-grandparents, etc. Each one of those branches into brothers and sisters, nieces and nephews, and other extended family members, and if you don't prioritize, you can easily find yourself going down a rabbit hole. (Honestly, those rabbit holes can be fun, but not necessarily productive.)

Researching your ancestry can take a long time. Set a reasonable deadline for accomplishing your objectives. Understand that learning about your family's past is a process that takes time and may include setbacks and unexpected findings. Setting aside a specific amount of time on particular days helps keep your priorities in order.

It is important to recognize the possible limitations of the records that are now accessible, particularly in light of historical events or natural disasters. When faced with knowledge gaps, this understanding helps reduce frustration and manage expectations. For example, in my research, I discovered that a large number of birth and marriage records were lost in a church fire in Temosachic, Chihuahua, Mexico, and as a result, one of my lines stops at the 3rd generation. It is what it is, and I have to move on.

Choose whether you wish to investigate a wider range of relatives or go in-depth with a select few ancestral lines. Depending on your time, available resources, and desired level of detail, you can strike a balance between the depth and breadth of your research.

Make use of the resources at hand. Determine the resources available to you, such as family records, online databases, archives, and libraries. Understanding where to get information makes conducting research easier and helps you accomplish your objectives more successfully. This guide will go into further detail on how to access databases, libraries, and archives. Your family records, if any, are always the best start.

There are frequently unanticipated turns in genealogy. Be ready to modify your expectations and goals in light of fresh facts. Being adaptable is essential for overcoming obstacles and taking advantage of learning opportunities.

Make sure you celebrate the small milestones in your research. Celebrate and give recognition to little victories along the way. Reaching a goal, like finishing a family tree branch or discovering a family history that you were unaware of, can inspire you and give you a sense of achievement.

Taking on the challenge of family research by yourself can be frustrating. Share your genealogy objectives with relatives or other researchers. By stating your goals, you can promote cooperation, rally support, and even facilitate the sharing of important information. Software like Ancestry.com allows you to collaborate with others to look for particular family lines.

Through deliberate goal-setting and expectation management, people can start their genealogy journey with direction and clarity. This method not only makes the research process more enjoyable and fulfilling, but it also makes it easier to

CHAPTER TWO - GETTING STARTED

discover the intricate web of one's family history.

Getting started with a family tree requires first obtaining some fundamental facts. Here's how to get important information from your close relatives and other accessible sources:

Start with the easiest source: speaking with close family members. Begin with your grandparents and parents. Request complete names, birthplaces, dates of birth, and maiden names for females. Ask relatives for anecdotes and tales about their forebears. Even though they're not always totally true, these tales might offer insightful suggestions for additional study. Often, with older family members, it is easier to get details from them by just asking simple questions. Using a simple recording device like your phone is an efficient way to gather information. This allows them to just talk about family members, significant events, cherished memories, and other items that go beyond simple birthdates and other statistical details. Once you review the recording, it allows you to go back and fill in the missing details.

As can be expected, I often find that as your relatives get older, their recall of specific dates and places can be a bit murky. Don't worry. The tools that I will show you can help you verify those details with a bit more specificity.

Gather details on your siblings, such as their birthplaces and dates of birth. You already may know some of that detail, but it does not hurt to verify. They can add information about spouses, kids, etc.

If possible, get copies of your parents', grandparents', and your birth, marriage, and death certificates. These documents frequently offer precise and thorough information. Family Bibles frequently include important details about marriages, births, and deaths. Verify whether your family has one and note any pertinent information.

Look through old family photos. They give us a visual link to our forefathers, but they could also feature writing on the back. Search for any papers, such as letters or diaries, that might have genealogy information. These might be in family archives or belong to elderly family members.

Get military records for your ancestors, if applicable. Discharge documents, service logs, and any honors or commendations are examples of these. Look through census data to learn more about family members. Every ten years, census records are made available and include information about names, ages, and relationships. Dates of birth and death can be obtained from Social Security data. For departed family members, request copies of their Social Security applications. For more information, look through public records such as wills, property records, and probate records.

This data is readily accessible in genealogy databases like MyHeritage, FamilySearch, and Ancestry.com. These platforms might already include records and family trees that can help you with your study.

For further information, get in touch with your aunts, uncles, and cousins. They might know specifics about family tree branches you are not as familiar with.

Whether you use genealogy software or paper records, don't forget to organize all of your information. You can gradually increase your understanding of your lineage by organizing the data you learn into a family tree as you accumulate more information.

3

Chapter Three - Putting Your Research in Order

"Organizing is what you do before you do something so that when you do it, it is not all mixed up." – A. A. Milne

It's a thrilling journey to set out on a journey to discover your family's past, but as your family tree grows, so does the need for effective organization. This chapter will address the essential techniques for becoming proficient in the field of genealogy organization so that your discoveries are not only significant but also painstakingly documented for future generations.

A. Create a Family Tree

1. Make use of software or online tools

The family tree, a graphic depiction of your lineage, is the foundation of every genealogy project. Family tree maintenance and creation have become easier than ever thanks to the variety of web resources and applications available in the digital era.

Ancestry.com, MyHeritage, and FamilySearch are just a few

of the websites that provide dynamic family tree building and exploration interfaces that are easy to use. By entering names, birthdates, marital status, and other important characteristics, you can use these tools to create a graphic map of your ancestry.

Select a platform that has tools for collaboration that fit your interests. For example, Ancestry.com lets you share your family tree with relatives and invites them to work with you on it.

2. Document Connections and Information

Recording names and dates are important, but so are the minute details that add character to your ancestors' stories as your family tree grows. Record connections, encapsulating the spirit of family bonds. Take note of the subtleties, such as migratory habits, jobs, and any inherited anecdotes.

To add context and personal anecdotes, make use of the notes and comments tools in the family tree program of your choice. With the addition of these particulars, your family tree will come to life as a dynamic history of your lineage.

B. Create a System for Filing

1. Arrange Pictures and Documents

A connection to the material remnants of your ancestors' history is what genealogy is all about—it's not just names on a chart. Arranging these records, which range from faded photos to birth certificates and letters, is essential to preserving the objectivity of your study.

For every ancestor, create physical or digital folders where documents are arranged either chronologically or thematically. To protect historic photos for future generations, digitize them, and don't forget to mark each file with relevant information.

It's all about consistency. Create a consistent file name system for your digital assets to make file retrieval simple. As an illustration, consider "Surname_Firstname_BirthCertificate_Year."

2. Maintain a Record of Citations and Sources

You must keep careful track of your sources while studying historical documents. Precise references not only confirm your results but also act as a guide for those who want to replicate your work.

Establish a mechanism for referencing references that includes the repository, the title of the document, page numbers, and the publishing date. Numerous genealogy software packages, such as Legacy Family Tree and RootsMagic, come with integrated tools for managing sources.

In summary, organizing your genealogy research is more than just a practical requirement; organizing your genealogy research is essential to maintaining and disseminating your family's history. Your filing system turns a pile of papers into a well-organized narrative, and the family tree becomes more than simply a diagram.

You are not just making a record for yourself when you painstakingly catalog relationships, facts, papers, and sources; you are also building the foundation for future generations. We'll delve into the abundance of information that lurks in libraries and archives in the upcoming chapter, and we'll walk you through the process of searching these repositories to find the undiscovered treasures from your family's past.

4

Chapter Four - Online Resources

"The digital revolution is far more significant than the invention of writing or even of printing." - **Douglas Engelbart**

Within the genealogy field, the digital environment represents previously uncharted territory with boundless potential. This chapter explores the vast array of internet resources and offers a thorough guide for anyone starting a family history project at any point. We'll look at ways to use the internet to uncover the mysteries of your family's past, from robust websites to lively social networks.

Look Through Genealogy Websites

The way we investigate our ancestry has been revolutionized by genealogy websites, among which FamilySearch, MyHeritage, and Ancestry.com are the most popular.

Embarking on a journey to trace your roots and build your family tree is an enriching experience, and several genealogy platforms offer valuable tools and resources to aid in this quest. Ancestry.com, MyHeritage.com, and FamilySearch are among

CHAPTER FOUR - ONLINE RESOURCES

the leading platforms, each bringing unique benefits to the table.

Ancestry.com

1. **Extensive Database:** Ancestry.com boasts an expansive database with over 27 million members and billions of historical records. This extensive collection includes census data, military records, immigration documents, and more, making it a powerful resource for comprehensive genealogical research.
2. **User-Friendly Interface:** Ancestry.com is known for its user-friendly interface, making it accessible to genealogy beginners and seasoned researchers alike. The platform's intuitive design simplifies the process of building and navigating family trees.
3. **DNA Testing Integration:** AncestryDNA, the DNA testing service offered by Ancestry.com, allows users to augment their research by uncovering ethnic origins and connecting with potential relatives. The seamless integration of DNA results with family trees enhances the overall genealogical experience.
4. **Collaborative Features:** Ancestry.com facilitates collaboration among researchers through shared family trees and the ability to connect with relatives who may be researching the same ancestors. This collaborative approach can lead to the discovery of new branches and insights.

MyHeritage.com

1. **Global Reach:** MyHeritage.com is celebrated for its global reach, offering access to records and archives

from around the world. This international perspective is particularly beneficial for individuals with diverse ancestral backgrounds.
2. **Smart Matching Technology:** MyHeritage employs Smart Matching technology, which automatically identifies potential matches between your family tree and others on the platform. This feature streamlines the discovery of shared ancestors and accelerates the building of comprehensive family trees.
3. **Photo Enhancement Tools:** MyHeritage stands out for its innovative photo enhancement tools. Through deep learning algorithms, the platform can colorize and enhance old family photos, bringing ancestral faces to life in vivid detail.
4. **Comprehensive Record Collections:** MyHeritage offers a vast collection of historical records, including census data, birth and marriage certificates, and immigration records. This wealth of information contributes to a more detailed understanding of your family's journey over generations.

FamilySearch

1. **Free Access to Records:** FamilySearch distinguishes itself by offering free access to an extensive array of historical records. This commitment to providing open access aligns with the platform's mission to make genealogical information freely available to the public.
2. **Collaborative and Non-Profit Approach:** FamilySearch operates as a non-profit organization, driven by a collaborative ethos. The platform encourages users to contribute to a shared global family tree, fostering a sense of commu-

nity and shared discovery.
3. **Research Guidance:** FamilySearch provides research guidance through online tutorials, webinars, and a robust Help Center. This educational focus supports users in honing their genealogical skills and navigating the complexities of ancestral research.

Access to Unique Collections: FamilySearch collaborates with archives and libraries globally, providing access to unique and diverse record collections. Researchers can explore records that may not be available on other platforms, expanding the scope of their genealogical investigations.

Whether you choose Ancestry.com, MyHeritage.com, or FamilySearch, each platform brings its own set of advantages to the table. MyHeritage, FamilySearch, and Ancestry.com can work in concert to provide a thorough method for learning about your ancestry The decision may depend on factors such as the geographical focus of your research, the specific tools and features that resonate with you, and your budget considerations. Ultimately, these platforms serve as invaluable companions on your journey to uncover the stories and connections that form the tapestry of your family history.

In addition to the three platforms listed above, several others might suit your particular needs. Those are listed in the resource section at the end of this book.

Think about subscribing to several platforms to optimize your research possibilities. Every service adds something special, enhancing the range and complexity of your family history research.

Make Use of Online Records and Databases

The extensive databases and documents that shed light on our ancestors' lives are the foundation of Internet genealogy research. The foundation of our family stories can be found in these digital treasures: marriage licenses, birth certificates, and military enlistments. Researchers can find a plethora of information by using websites such as ArchiveGrid and Cyndi's List, which serve as virtual portals to a multitude of online data.

Learn how to do sophisticated searches in various databases. To improve your results, try different names, dates, and locations together. The effectiveness of your searches can have a big impact on how quickly and in-depth your research is.

Forums and Social Networks

In the era of social media, genealogy clubs on sites like Facebook have evolved into online town squares where researchers congregate to exchange ideas, get guidance, and celebrate findings. Organizations like "DNA Detectives" and "Genealogy Enthusiasts Worldwide" provide lively discussion boards for people of all skill levels. By participating in these communities, you can connect with like-minded researchers and discover new opportunities for collaboration.

Engage in lively conversation in groups. Ask questions, discuss your research, and interact with people. These internet networks' collaborative nature frequently results in discoveries and unforeseen relationships.

Establish Contact with Other Scholars

The collective experiences and knowledge of other researchers enhance the process of discovering your family history. There are places for in-depth conversations and information exchange on online forums such as RootsWeb, GenForum, and the Geneal-

CHAPTER FOUR - ONLINE RESOURCES

ogy Stack Exchange. Interacting with other enthusiasts offers new insights into your work, as well as access to shared family trees and possible partners.

Never be afraid to ask for advice or to discuss difficulties you've had. Making connections with seasoned genealogists might offer helpful research shortcuts and insights.

The combination of technology and genealogy in this digital age has led to an unprecedented period of discovery. With each online click, search, and interaction, we get one step closer to piecing together the complex history of our families. To reconnect with your ancestry, "Tracing Ancestry" challenges you to traverse this digital frontier and make use of the abundance of resources at your disposal.

As you set out on your virtual adventure, keep in mind that every document you look over and every connection you make adds to the story of your family. The upcoming chapter will lead you into the sacred corridors of libraries and archives, where priceless finds are waiting to be unearthed. Modern web resources combined with tried-and-true research techniques create a powerful symbiotic relationship that will enable you to take on the role of family historian.

5

Chapter Five - Visiting Archives and Libraries

"The only thing that you have to know is the location of the library."
— **Albert Einstein**

As we delve deeper into the labyrinth of genealogical exploration, our next frontier lies within the hallowed halls of archives and libraries. In this chapter, we will navigate the landscape of these repositories, guiding you on a journey to unearth the hidden treasures that reside in local archives and expansive national collections.

Visit Local Archives and Libraries

Local archives and libraries are the bedrock of genealogical research, offering a wealth of resources that intimately connect you to the roots of your community. Paying a visit to these repositories is akin to stepping into a time capsule, where documents, newspapers, and artifacts whisper the stories of

CHAPTER FIVE - VISITING ARCHIVES AND LIBRARIES

those who walked the same streets and lived in the same neighborhoods as your ancestors.

Start by identifying local archives and libraries in your area. Municipal libraries, county archives, and historical societies often house collections of vital records, newspapers, maps, and local histories. Plan your visit ahead of time, checking their catalog and contacting archivists or librarians to ensure the availability of relevant materials.

Family Search Libraries are available at many buildings of the Church of Jesus Christ of Latter-Day Saints. At FamilySearch centers, local volunteers offer a range of services, including personalized guidance on family history research techniques and FamilySearch usage. The Internet, computers, and premium family history websites are all complimentary. (The available materials vary by locality.). They also provide access to historical records and photographs that are restricted to centers.

Although every center is different, they all provide a place to find out more about your ancestors. There are centers in a variety of structures, including churches and libraries. You can find the nearest Family Search Library at https://locations.familysearch.org/en.

Attend any workshops or events hosted by these local institutions. Engaging with the local genealogical community can provide insights into resources and methodologies specific to your area.

Access Regional Records and Documents

Once you've tapped into local resources, extend your reach to regional records and documents. Many states and provinces maintain archives that hold a trove of information relevant to broader geographical areas. Explore census records, land deeds, wills, and other regional documents that offer a panoramic view of your ancestors' lives.

Dive into regional newspapers, which can be invaluable in uncovering historical events, social trends, and even personal anecdotes. Online catalogs and finding aids provided by archives will assist you in identifying relevant materials before your visit.

Collaborate with local genealogy or historical societies. Their expertise and familiarity with regional resources can provide shortcuts and insights into navigating local and regional archives effectively.

National Archives
Explore Government Records

The National Archives, the custodians of government records, open up a treasure chest of information spanning various aspects of your ancestors' lives. Whether military service, immigration, or federal census data, these archives provide a panoramic view of your family's journey through time.

Researching government records often involves a blend of physical visits and online exploration. Identify the national archive that houses the records pertinent to your research. Familiarize yourself with their online databases and digital collections, and when possible, plan a visit to access materials that may not be available digitally.

Make use of online finding aids and guides provided by national archives. They can help you navigate the extensive collections and streamline your research process.

Utilize Historical Archives

Beyond government records, historical archives hold an eclectic array of materials that breathe life into your genealogical narrative. Manuscripts, diaries, photographs, and ephemera

CHAPTER FIVE - VISITING ARCHIVES AND LIBRARIES

can unveil personal stories and provide context to the broader historical landscape in which your ancestors lived. A list of genealogical archives is listed in the appendix.

Explore the holdings of historical societies, university archives, and specialized repositories. Many of these institutions offer online catalogs and digitized collections, allowing you to conduct preliminary research from the comfort of your home.

Leverage the expertise of archivists. When planning a visit, reach out to the archival staff with specific inquiries. Their knowledge of the collections can guide you to hidden gems that align with your research goals.

Visiting archives and libraries is a pilgrimage for genealogists, a journey through time that bridges the gap between the past and the present. Local repositories offer an intimate connection to community histories, while national and historical archives unravel the broader tapestry of your family's story.

When planning a genealogical research trip, it's advisable to check the specific resources and policies of each archive. Additionally, online access to many archives and their collections has become more prevalent, allowing researchers to explore valuable resources remotely.

As you embark on these expeditions, remember to approach each visit with preparation and reverence. Respect the rules and regulations of the archives, take meticulous notes, and document your findings. In the next chapter, we will explore the power of DNA testing in genealogy, unlocking genetic clues that can enrich and validate your research and provide a holistic view of your familial legacy.

6

Chapter Six - DNA Testing

Genes are like the story, and DNA is the language that the story is written in. Sam Kean

In the ever-evolving landscape of genealogy, the advent of DNA testing has ushered in a revolutionary era. In this chapter, we'll embark on a journey into the realm of genetic exploration, exploring the introduction, selection, and interpretation of DNA testing for genealogy.

Genealogical DNA testing involves analyzing particular DNA segments to provide information on a person's ethnic makeup, ancestry, and kin relationships. This investigation goes beyond customary paper trails, providing an exact and scientific way to find family connections that may have been lost to time.

This guide is not intended to provide a complete scientific explanation of DNA testing. A short, concise explanation of the kinds of DNA tests that are used follows.

Y-DNA, autosomal, and mitochondrial DNA (mtDNA) testing are the three main kinds of DNA tests used in genealogy.

CHAPTER SIX - DNA TESTING

- Y-DNA testing: This method follows the father's lineage from son to son.
- mtDNA testing: passed from mother to both sons and daughters, it traces the maternal line.
- Autosomal DNA testing: Offers a more comprehensive picture of an individual's genetic background by analyzing DNA from all ancestors.

Creating a DNA testing plan appropriate to your genealogical aims requires an understanding of the limitations and specific goals of each test.

Selecting a DNA Testing Service

Embarking on a journey to discover one's genetic heritage has become a transformative experience, unlocking the secrets hidden within our DNA. Several DNA testing sites have emerged as leaders in this field, each offering unique benefits that contribute to a deeper understanding of our ancestry, health, and familial connections. The primary DNA testing sites—23andMe, AncestryDNA, and MyHeritageDNA—stand out for their comprehensive offerings, innovative features, and the potential to unearth hidden aspects of our genetic makeup.

23andMe

1. Ancestry Composition:

One of the defining features of 23andMe is its detailed ancestry composition report. Users receive a breakdown of their genetic heritage, highlighting the percentage of DNA associated with different populations around the world. This provides a vivid picture of one's ancestral origins and migration patterns.

2. Health and Wellness Insights:
23andMe goes beyond ancestry by offering health-related insights. The platform provides information on genetic predispositions to certain health conditions, carrier status for inherited conditions, and responses to certain medications. This multifaceted approach provides a holistic view of both genetic ancestry and potential health risks.

3. DNA Relatives:
The DNA Relatives feature allows users to connect with individuals who share a portion of their DNA. This can lead to the discovery of previously unknown relatives, fostering connections, and expanding one's family network. Users can opt to share as much or as little information as they feel comfortable with.

4. Research Participation:
23andMe offers users the opportunity to contribute to genetic research by participating in studies. This collaborative research approach allows individuals to actively contribute to scientific advancements while gaining a deeper understanding of their genetic makeup.

AncestryDNA

1. Massive DNA Database:
AncestryDNA boasts one of the largest DNA databases in the world, with millions of users. This extensive pool of genetic data enhances the likelihood of finding relatives and building a comprehensive family tree.

2. Thorough Historical Insights:
AncestryDNA provides rich historical insights through its Genetic Communities feature. Users can explore connections to specific geographical and cultural groups, gaining a deeper understanding of their family's historical context.

3. Integrated Family Tree Building:
AncestryDNA seamlessly integrates with Ancestry.com's genealogy platform, allowing users to build and expand their family trees based on DNA matches. This integrated approach connects genetic data with historical records, enriching the narrative of one's family history.

4. Dynamic Matching Algorithm:
AncestryDNA employs a dynamic matching algorithm that continually updates as more users join the platform. This ensures that users receive the most accurate and relevant DNA matches over time, facilitating ongoing discoveries.

MyHeritageDNA

1. Global DNA Matches:
MyHeritageDNA offers a global perspective on genetic connections, with a substantial user base from diverse regions. This broad reach increases the likelihood of discovering relatives from various parts of the world.

2. DNA Matching with Family Trees:
The extensive collection of family trees available on MyHeritageDNA complements its DNA-matching feature. This dual approach enhances the chances of making meaningful

connections by aligning genetic data with documented family histories.

3. Chromosome Browser:
MyHeritageDNA provides a Chromosome Browser tool, allowing users to visualize and explore shared DNA segments with their matches. This advanced feature provides a deeper level of insight into genetic connections and shared ancestries.

4. Inclusive Ethnicity Estimates:
MyHeritageDNA's ethnicity estimates encompass a wide range of ethnicities, including smaller and more specific population groups. This inclusivity adds granularity to ancestral insights, offering a nuanced perspective on one's genetic heritage.

When selecting a DNA testing service, consider your research goals, budget, and the scope of genetic genealogy tools each company offers. It's often beneficial to explore multiple testing services to maximize your chances of finding genetic matches and uncovering diverse ancestral connections.

Stay informed about updates and advancements in genetic testing technology. The landscape is continually evolving, with companies enhancing their algorithms and expanding their databases.

Understanding and Interpreting DNA Results

Upon receiving your DNA results, a new chapter of exploration unfolds. Understanding and interpreting these results requires a blend of scientific knowledge and genealogical acumen.

Ethnicity Estimates

Most DNA testing services provide ethnicity estimates, out-

CHAPTER SIX - DNA TESTING

lining the geographical regions associated with your genetic makeup. While these estimates offer valuable insights into your ancestral origins, it's crucial to interpret them with a nuanced perspective. Genetic admixture, migration patterns, and historical events can all influence the composition of your ethnicity estimates.

DNA Matches

DNA matching is a cornerstone of genetic genealogy. When you receive a list of DNA matches, each represents a potential relative with shared genetic material. Understanding the degree of relatedness (e.g., close family, distant cousin) and exploring shared segments of DNA can unlock new branches of your family tree.

Haplogroups

Y-DNA and mtDNA testing reveal haplogroups, providing information about your paternal and maternal ancestral lines, respectively. Haplogroups trace the migratory patterns of ancient ancestors and offer a deep dive into the deep roots of your genetic heritage.

Genetic Health Insights (where applicable)

Some DNA testing services, like 23andMe, provide health-related genetic insights. While these details can offer valuable information about potential health risks, it's essential to approach such results with caution and consult with healthcare professionals for comprehensive guidance.

Collaborate with your DNA matches. Engaging in communication, comparing family trees, and sharing information can lead to collaborative breakthroughs in your genealogical research.

Conclusion

DNA testing adds a dynamic and scientific dimension to your

genealogical journey, unraveling ancestral threads that stretch across continents and centuries. As we navigate the genetic terrain, remember that each result is a piece of a larger puzzle—an invitation to explore, connect, and rediscover your familial heritage.

In the next chapter, we'll delve into overcoming challenges in genealogy research. From missing records to conflicting information, these hurdles are an inherent part of the journey. By equipping yourself with strategies and resilience, you'll navigate through the complexities and continue to unveil the stories woven into your family's tapestry.

7

Chapter Seven - Overcoming Challenges

"Some fish love to swim upstream. Some people love to overcome challenges."
— **Amit Ray, Walking the Path of Compassion**

In the pursuit of unraveling the intricate tapestry of one's family history, genealogists often encounter a myriad of challenges. From elusive ancestors to conflicting information that tests the boundaries of certainty, these obstacles can at times seem insurmountable. However, as seasoned researchers will attest, the key lies not just in navigating these challenges but in embracing them as integral parts of the genealogical journey.

A. Common Obstacles in Genealogy Research

1. Missing or Incomplete Records

The genealogical quest is frequently hindered by the absence or incompleteness of records. Vital documents such as birth certificates, marriage records, or census data may be lost to time, natural disasters, or bureaucratic inefficiencies. This scarcity can create frustrating roadblocks in the pursuit of an unbroken family lineage.

Strategies for Addressing Missing or Incomplete Records:

- **Alternative Sources:** Seek out alternative sources of information, such as church records, military records, or local archives. In some cases, indirect sources like newspaper articles or land deeds may hold crucial details.
- **Collaborative Efforts:** Engage with local historical societies and genealogy groups. These organizations often know obscure or overlooked records that can aid in filling gaps.

2. Dealing with Conflicting Information

Conflicting information is an inherent challenge in genealogy, arising from discrepancies in historical records, oral family traditions, or varying interpretations of available data. Resolving these conflicts requires a delicate balancing act between thorough research and a discerning eye for accuracy.

Strategies for Addressing Conflicting Information:

- **Source Evaluation:** Scrutinize the reliability of sources. Primary sources, or contemporary records created at the time of the event, are generally more reliable than secondary sources or family anecdotes.
- **Corroboration:** Cross-reference information from multiple sources to identify patterns and commonalities. Consistency across various records increases the likelihood of accuracy.

B. Strategies for Overcoming Challenges

1. Collaboration with Other Researchers

Genealogy is inherently a collaborative endeavor. Sharing insights, discoveries, and challenges with fellow researchers can be immensely beneficial in overcoming obstacles. The collective knowledge of a community often unveils new perspectives and untapped resources.

Effective Strategies for Collaborative Genealogy:

- **Join Genealogy Groups:** Participate in genealogy forums, social media groups, or local genealogy societies. These platforms provide opportunities to connect with experienced researchers, share challenges, and seek advice.
- **Collaborative Research Projects:** Engage in collaborative research projects with other genealogists who may have complementary skills or expertise. Pooling resources and insights can lead to breakthroughs in challenging cases.
- **Crowdsourced Transcription:** Contribute to or leverage crowdsourced transcription projects. Many genealogy websites host initiatives where volunteers transcribe historical documents, making them more accessible to researchers.

2. Persistence and Patience

Genealogy is a journey that requires tenacity, as breakthroughs often come to those who persevere. The process of piecing together a family's history can be arduous, with twists and turns that demand not only research skills but also resilience in the face of setbacks.

Strategies for Cultivating Persistence and Patience:

- **Set realistic expectations.** Recognize that genealogical breakthroughs may take time. Setting realistic expectations prevents frustration and allows for a more sustainable approach to research.
- **Celebrate Small Victories:** Acknowledge and celebrate

incremental victories, no matter how small. Each piece of information uncovered contributes to the larger mosaic of family history.
- **Take Breaks When Needed:** Genealogy can be all-consuming. Taking breaks when faced with challenges can provide fresh perspectives upon return. Stepping back for a while can sometimes lead to breakthroughs when you least expect them.

Conclusion

In the realm of genealogy, overcoming challenges is not just a necessity but a rite of passage. The pursuit of elusive ancestors and the deciphering of conflicting information are woven into the fabric of the genealogical journey. Embracing these challenges with a strategic mindset, a collaborative spirit, and unwavering patience distinguishes the seasoned genealogist from the novice.

As you navigate the twists and turns of your family's history, remember that every roadblock is an opportunity for growth and discovery. Collaborate with fellow researchers, cultivate patience, and persist in the face of adversity.

In the next chapter of this guide, we will discuss the significance of keeping your family tree and other genealogical records. The journey does not end with uncovering the past; rather, it concludes with making sure that the stories of your ancestors continue to reverberate through the ages. This includes everything from establishing a family archive to communicating your discoveries to subsequent generations.

8

Chapter 8 - Preserving Family History

"Remember me in the family tree; my name, my days, my strife. Then I'll ride upon the wings of time and live an endless life" —Linda Goetsch

As the custodian of your family's past, the responsibility to preserve and share its history is both a privilege and a duty. In this chapter, we will explore the multifaceted approach to preserving family history, encompassing the creation of a family archive through the digitization of photographs and documents, the art of crafting family stories and narratives, and the significance of sharing these findings with relatives through avenues such as family reunions, websites, or newsletters.

A. Creating a Family Archive

1. Digitizing Photographs and Documents

The fragility of physical artifacts underscores the importance of digitization in preserving family history. Digitizing photographs and documents not only safeguards these treasures from the passage of time but also facilitates easy sharing and accessibility for generations to come.

Steps for Digitizing Your Family Archive:

1. Organize Materials: Before embarking on the digitization journey, organize your materials. Group photographs and documents by theme, era, or family branch.
2. Invest in Quality Scanning Equipment: A high-quality scanner is essential for preserving the integrity of your photographs and documents. Consider the type of items you'll be scanning and choose a scanner with appropriate specifications.
3. Adjust Scanning Settings: Customize scanning settings based on the nature of each item. Photographs may require higher resolutions, while documents may be adequately captured at lower resolutions.
4. Organize Digital Files: Create a digital filing system mirroring the organization of your physical materials. Clearly label folders and use descriptive filenames for individual files. This structured approach enhances accessibility.
5. Implement a Backup Strategy: The digital archive is as vulnerable as its physical counterpart. Regularly back up your digital files using external hard drives, cloud storage, or a combination of both to prevent data loss.

2. Writing Family Stories and Narratives

While photographs and documents provide a visual and factual snapshot of the past, family stories, and narratives breathe life into these historical records. Crafting compelling narratives transforms your ancestors from names on a family tree into vibrant characters with lived experiences.

CHAPTER 8 - PRESERVING FAMILY HISTORY

Approaches to Writing Family Stories:

1. Chronological Storytelling: Organize your narratives chronologically, starting with the earliest known ancestors and progressing through the generations. This approach provides a cohesive timeline of your family's journey.
2. Thematic Narratives: Explore specific themes or aspects of your family history. This could include stories of resilience, migration, or cultural traditions that have been passed down through generations.
3. Individual Profiles: Create detailed profiles for significant ancestors. Highlight their achievements, challenges, and unique characteristics. This personal touch adds depth to your family narratives.

Writing Tips for Compelling Narratives:

- Immersive Descriptions: Transport your readers to different eras and locations through vivid descriptions of the settings and contexts in which your ancestors lived.

- Emotional Connections: Evoke emotions by delving into the joys, triumphs, and even sorrows that have shaped your family's narrative. Emotional connections resonate with readers and make the stories more relatable.

- Incorporate Historical Context: Place your family's story within the broader context of historical events. This not only enriches the narrative but also provides a valuable educational component for future generations.

Invite Collaboration: Encourage family members to contribute their own stories and perspectives. Collaborative storytelling not only broadens the scope of your family history but also fosters a sense of shared ownership.

B. Sharing Findings with Relatives

1. Hosting Family Reunions

Family reunions serve as vibrant celebrations of shared heritage and provide the perfect platform to disseminate your findings. These gatherings foster a sense of connection among relatives, bridging generational gaps and reinforcing the importance of family history.

Strategies for Hosting Family Reunions:

1. Incorporate Genealogy Activities: Integrate genealogy-themed activities into the reunion agenda. This could include storytelling sessions, photo exhibits, or even collaborative family tree-building.
2. Create a Presentation: Prepare a captivating presentation summarizing key findings from your research. Use visuals, anecdotes, and historical context to engage your audience.
3. Engage Younger Generations: Make the event inclusive for younger family members. Consider organizing games, scavenger hunts, or interactive activities that convey family history in an accessible and entertaining manner.

2. Creating a Family Website or Newsletter

In our digital age, disseminating information has never been easier. A family website or newsletter acts as a virtual repository, accessible to family members across geographical boundaries.

Steps for Creating a Family Website or Newsletter:

1. Select a Platform: Choose a user-friendly platform for your family website or newsletter. Platforms like WordPress, Wix, or Squarespace offer customizable templates and easy-to-use interfaces.

2. Organize Content: Structure your website or newsletter with sections dedicated to family history, stories, photographs, and updates. Keep the layout intuitive for easy navigation.
3. Incorporate Multimedia: Include photographs, scanned documents, and multimedia elements to enhance the visual appeal of your digital platform. These elements bring your family history to life.
4. Regular Updates: Commit to regular updates to keep the content fresh. Share discoveries, stories, and any contributions from family members.
5. Encourage Interaction: Include features that encourage interaction, such as comment sections, forums, or a shared family calendar. A collaborative digital space fosters ongoing engagement.

Conclusion

Preserving and sharing family history is a holistic endeavor that combines the meticulous archiving of tangible artifacts with the artful storytelling of ancestral narratives. From the digitization of photographs and documents to the creation of family websites and newsletters, each element contributes to the legacy that you pass down through generations.

9

Chapter 9 - Continuing Education

In any given moment we have two options: to step forward into growth or to step back into safety. -Abraham Maslow

When it comes to the ever-changing environment of genealogy, the journey to uncover the histories of one's family is both a timeless exploration and a modern adventure. To ensure that genealogists can navigate the broad landscape of family history with the appropriate skills and expertise, continuing education offers the compass that guides them through the complexities of this fascinating pursuit.

A. Participate in Genealogy Workshops and National Conferences

Genealogy conferences and workshops serve as pillars of information, providing enthusiasts with a priceless opportunity to immerse themselves in the most recent developments, approaches, and discoveries that have been made in the field of genealogy. These events, which are frequently packed with seasoned academics, specialists, and others who share simi-

CHAPTER 9 - CONTINUING EDUCATION

lar interests, offer a venue that is conducive to learning and collaboration, which is very beneficial.

During these get-togethers, attendees delve into a wide variety of subjects, ranging from cutting-edge research methods to the application of cutting-edge technology in genealogical endeavors. Participants have the chance to gain practical experience during workshops run by experienced professionals, which enables them to hone their skills and put new techniques into practice in real-time.

The practice of attending genealogy conferences not only helps one have a deeper understanding of the field but also helps one feel more connected to the community. Creating a dynamic learning environment that goes beyond the pages of historical documents can be accomplished by interacting with other enthusiasts, sharing experiences, and exchanging insights.

Make sure that you are up to date on the newest research methods and tools. In the field of genealogy, which is undergoing rapid advancement, a researcher needs to be current on the latest research methodologies and tools to maintain their level of success. The environment of family history research is continually being reimagined as a result of technological advancements, digital databases, and better analytical techniques. By embracing these changes, genealogists are provided with the tools necessary to decipher intricate genealogies and uncover previously concealed narratives.

Embracing DNA Technology: The use of DNA testing has completely transformed the field of genealogy research, providing insights into the origins and connections of ancestors that were previously unattainable. Modern genealogists need to have a comprehensive understanding of the complexities of

DNA testing services, the ability to interpret the results, and awareness of the latest developments in this field.

Using Online Platforms: In this day and age, when the digital world is in full swing, the utilization of online platforms is of utmost importance in the field of genealogy research. Increasing the effectiveness of research attempts can be accomplished by maintaining current knowledge of the most recent features offered by genealogical websites such as Ancestry.com and MyHeritage. Researchers need to have a working knowledge of these platforms to fully exploit their potential.

Incorporating Social Media: Genealogists are increasingly leveraging social media platforms for networking and working together. Through participation in Twitter conversations or joining genealogy groups on social media platforms such as Facebook, one can gain access to the opportunity to collaborate with researchers from all over the world, share their experiences, and benefit from their advice.

Techniques for the Preservation of Data: As technology advances, so do the methods currently available for the preservation of genealogical data. Not only does familiarity with digital archiving, cloud storage, and metadata management ensure that valuable family history documents are identified, but it also ensures that these records are maintained for future generations.

Learning new skills is only one aspect of continuing education; it also involves cultivating a mindset that is open to change and curious about the world around you. Genealogists are encouraged to approach their research with a forward-looking mindset, ready to embrace the innovations that will influence the future of family history discovery. This has the effect of encouraging genealogists to be more open to new ideas.

CHAPTER 9 - CONTINUING EDUCATION

During the process of uncovering one's roots, education serves as a compass that points toward new horizons. It leads genealogists into unexplored territory and connects them with the vast amount of information that is waiting to be discovered. The commitment to ongoing learning becomes the cornerstone of a meaningful and fascinating inquiry into the intricate tapestry of our familial past as we navigate the ever-changing terrain of genealogy. This is because the landscape of genealogy is constantly shifting.

In the concluding chapter of this guide, we will reflect on the profound impact of your genealogical journey. From the lessons learned to the bridges built with relatives, your dedication to uncovering and preserving family history is a gift that transcends time.

10

Chapter 10 - Reflections and Gratitude

"I think gratitude is a big thing. It puts you in a place where you're humble." **Andra Day**

As we reach the culmination of this journey, it's time to reflect on the profound impact of uncovering and preserving family history. The threads of our ancestors, once obscured by the veil of time, have been meticulously woven into a rich tapestry—a legacy that transcends generations. Let us pause and consider the lessons learned, the stories shared, and the bridges built with relatives near and far.

A. The Profound Impact of the Genealogical Journey

The pursuit of family history is not merely an academic exercise or a journey through dusty archives; it is an odyssey of self-discovery. In retracing the steps of our forebears, we have unearthed not only names and dates but also the resilience, triumphs, and stories that define us. We've connected with the echoes of our ancestors, understanding that their struggles and triumphs continue to shape our identities.

CHAPTER 10 - REFLECTIONS AND GRATITUDE

As we stand on the threshold between the past and the present, the lessons gleaned from our genealogical journey extend beyond the pages of documents and family trees. We carry forward the virtues of resilience, curiosity, and the importance of preserving stories that might otherwise be lost to time.

B. Bridges Built and Relationships Nurtured

Genealogy is a bridge that spans generations, bringing families closer together. Through family reunions, shared narratives, and collaborative efforts, we have strengthened the bonds that tie us to our relatives. The warmth of familial connections has transcended the boundaries of time and space, creating a sense of belonging that enriches our lives.

In connecting with relatives, whether through shared stories or the exchange of information, we've become part of a living legacy. The stories we've uncovered are not static; they are alive in the conversations, traditions, and shared memories of family members. Through our efforts, we've become the custodians of these narratives, passing them down to future generations.

C. The Endurance of Family Legacy

As we conclude this chapter of our shared exploration, let us not forget that our journey is a continuous one. The family history we've meticulously curated and preserved is a gift that endures, carrying the torch of our ancestral legacy into the future. It is a living testament to the resilience of the human spirit and the enduring power of familial connections.

D. Gratitude and a Request for Reflection

I extend my deepest gratitude to each reader who embarked on this journey through time and heritage. Your commitment to uncovering family history is not only a testament to your curiosity but also a contribution to the collective narrative of human history.

As you close this book, I invite you to take a moment for reflection. Consider the stories that resonated with you, the discoveries that sparked your curiosity, and the connections you've forged with your family history. Your feedback is invaluable in shaping the future editions of this guide.

If this book has enriched your understanding of family history and inspired you to embark on your genealogical journey, I kindly ask for your support. A positive review would not only be a testament to the impact of this guide but also a beacon for others seeking to explore the tapestry of their ancestral roots.

May the echoes of your ancestors continue to guide and inspire you as you navigate the intricate threads of your family history. As the keeper of your familial legacy, you contribute to a story that transcends time—a story that continues to be written with each passing generation.

Thank you for being a part of this shared odyssey through the tapestry of family history.

With heartfelt gratitude,
  Randy L. Bullis

11

APPENDIX

RESOURCES TO HELP YOU WITH YOUR FAMILY HISTORY QUEST

There are several genealogy software programs available to help individuals organize, research, and document their family history. Here's a list of some popular genealogy software:

Family Tree Maker:

Family Tree Maker is a standalone genealogy software that allows users to create, edit, and organize their family trees. It offers features like charting, reporting, and integration with online services.

Legacy Family Tree:

Legacy Family Tree is a comprehensive genealogy software with features for managing family trees, recording sources, and creating reports. It also offers integration with online databases.

Gramps (Free and Open Source):

Gramps is an open-source genealogy software that is free to

use. It provides a variety of tools for managing family trees, tracking relationships, and generating reports.

MyHeritage Family Tree Builder:
MyHeritage's Family Tree Builder is a free genealogy software that allows users to create, edit, and share family trees. It integrates with MyHeritage's online database.

RootsMagic:
RootsMagic is a user-friendly genealogy software that supports the creation and management of family trees. It offers features like source documentation, report generation, and integration with online databases.

Heredis:
Heredis is a genealogy software that offers tools for building family trees, recording events, and managing multimedia. It supports synchronization with online databases.

Ancestral Quest:
Ancestral Quest is a genealogy software with features for creating and editing family trees, tracking sources, and generating reports. It also supports integration with FamilySearch.

GenoPro:
GenoPro is a unique genealogy software that specializes in creating visual family trees. It provides features for adding photos, generating detailed reports, and creating interactive family tree charts.

Family Historian:

Family Historian is a genealogy software that emphasizes ease of use and visualization. It supports the creation of family trees, recording events, and generating charts and reports.

TribalPages:
TribalPages is both an online family tree hosting service and genealogy software. Users can create, edit, and manage family trees, and then share them online with family members.

Clooz:
Clooz is a specialized genealogy software that focuses on organizing and analyzing historical documents. It assists in the extraction and categorization of information from various records.

There are several free genealogy tools available to help you in your quest to discover your family history. Here's a list of free genealogy tools that you can explore:

GEDmatch:
GEDmatch is a free online tool that allows users to compare and analyze their DNA test results from various testing companies.

WikiTree:
WikiTree is a free, collaborative family tree website where members work together to create a single worldwide family tree.

Find A Grave:
Find A Grave is a free online resource for locating and documenting cemetery records. Users can contribute by adding grave

records and photographs.

RootsWeb:
RootsWeb provides free access to genealogy resources, including message boards, mailing lists, and user-contributed family trees.

TNGenWeb:
TNGenWeb is part of the USGenWeb project, providing free genealogy resources specific to Tennessee, including census data, military records, and more.

Access Genealogy:
Access Genealogy offers a wealth of free genealogy resources, including census records, Native American records, and military records.

FreeCEN:
FreeCEN provides free access to transcriptions of 19th-century UK census records, allowing users to search and explore census data.

HeritageQuest Online (Accessible via Libraries):
Many public libraries offer free access to HeritageQuest Online, a database with census records, family histories, and other genealogy resources.

Chronicling America: Historic American Newspapers:
Chronicling America is a free resource from the Library of Congress that provides access to digitized historic American newspapers.

Open Archives:
Open Archives is a Dutch genealogy website that provides free access to a variety of historical records, including birth, marriage, and death records.

Daughters of the American Revolution (DAR) Genealogical Research System:
The DAR Genealogical Research System offers free access to a database of genealogical records related to individuals who contributed to American independence.

USGenWeb Project:
USGenWeb is a volunteer-driven project offering free genealogy resources and information for every U.S. state and county.

BillionGraves:
BillionGraves is a free platform for documenting and preserving cemetery records through crowdsourced efforts.

Genealogical research often involves exploring archives and repositories that house historical records. Across the United States, there are numerous archives and institutions dedicated to preserving and providing access to genealogical resources. Here is a list of notable genealogical archives across the USA:

1. **National Archives and Records Administration (NARA)**

   - *Location:* Multiple locations, including Washington, D.C., and regional branches.
   - *Website:* National Archives

1. **Library of Congress - Local History and Genealogy Reading Room**

   - *Location:* Washington, D.C.
   - *Website:* Library of Congress - Genealogy

1. **New England Historic Genealogical Society (NEHGS)**

   - *Location:* Boston, Massachusetts
   - *Website:* NEHGS

1. **Family History Library**

   - *Location:* Salt Lake City, Utah
   - *Website:* FamilySearch - Family History Library

1. **Allen County Public Library - Genealogy Center**

   - *Location:* Fort Wayne, Indiana
   - *Website:* ACPL Genealogy Center

1. **New York Public Library - Milstein Division of United States History, Local History, and Genealogy**

   - *Location:* New York, New York
   - *Website:* NYPL - Milstein Division

1. **Daughters of the American Revolution (DAR) Library**

   - *Location:* Washington, D.C.
   - *Website:* DAR Library

APPENDIX

1. **State Archives and Libraries:**

- Many states have their own archives and libraries with extensive genealogical collections. Examples include the Georgia Archives, Pennsylvania State Archives, and California State Archives.

1. **Midwest Genealogy Center**

- *Location:* Independence, Missouri
- *Website:* Midwest Genealogy Center

1. **Kentucky Historical Society – Martin F. Schmidt Research Library**

- *Location:* Frankfort, Kentucky
- *Website:* Kentucky Historical Society

1. **Southern California Genealogical Society – Genealogy Library**

- *Location:* Burbank, California
- *Website:* SCGS Library

1. **Minnesota Historical Society – Gale Family Library**

- *Location:* St. Paul, Minnesota
- *Website:* MHS – Gale Family Library

1. **Virginia Historical Society – Library**

- *Location:* Richmond, Virginia
- *Website:* Virginia Historical Society

1. **Ohio History Connection - Archives/Library**

- *Location:* Columbus, Ohio
- *Website:* Ohio History Connection

1. **Mississippi Department of Archives and History - Archives and Library**

- *Location:* Jackson, Mississippi
- *Website:* MDAH Archives and Library

Made in the USA
Middletown, DE
15 September 2024

60993258R00035